seals

BY KARA L. LAUGHLIN

The Child's World®
childsworld.com

Published by The Child's World®
1980 Lookout Drive • Mankato, MN 56003-1705
800-599-READ • www.childsworld.com

DESIGN ELEMENTS
© creatOR76/Shutterstock.com: porthole
© keren-seg/Shutterstock.com: water

PHOTO CREDITS
© Eric Isselee/Shutterstock.com: cover, 1; Ethan Daniels/
Shutterstock.com: 5; IanC66/Shutterstock.com: 20-21; KarynJ/
Shutterstock.com: 8-9; mb-fotos/iStockphoto.com: 14-15; Nicram
Sabod/Shutterstock.com: 12-13; Soygirl53/Shutterstock.com: 18-
19; Tom Middleton/Shutterstock.com: 17; Wollertz/Shutterstock.
com: 11; zaferkizilkaya/Shutterstock.com: 6-7

ISBN: 9781503816916
LCCN: 2016945607

Printed in the United States of America
PA02326

NOTE FOR PARENTS AND TEACHERS

The Child's World® helps early readers develop their
informational-reading skills by providing easy-to-read books
that fascinate them and hold their interest. Encourage new
readers by following these simple ideas:

BEFORE READING

- Page briefly through the book. Discuss the photos. What
  does the reader think he or she will learn in this book? Let
  the child ask questions.
- Look at the glossary together. Discuss the words.

READ THE BOOK

- Now read the book together, or let the child read the book
  independently.

AFTER READING

- Urge the child to think more. Ask questions such as, "What
  things are different among the animals shown in this book?"

Contents

Seals by the Sea

What are those animals on the rocks? They are seals.

Seals live all over the world. They live in the water and on land.

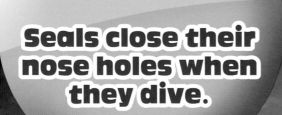

Did you know?

Seals close their nose holes when they dive.

Flippers and Fur

Seals do not have feet. They have **flippers**. Flippers help seals swim and turn. Seals are fast swimmers.

Seals are covered in fur. The fur is waterproof.

did you know?

Seals have fat under their skin to keep them warm.

Did you know?

Seals and sea lions are not the same. They are different animals.

Molting

Once a year, a seal sheds its old skin and fur. This is called **molting**. Molting does not hurt the seals. New fur is ready underneath!

On Land

Seals stay in groups called **herds**. When herds move from the sea to the land, they **haul-out**.

Seals haul-out to rest, molt, and have babies.

Did you know?

One herd can have hundreds of seals.

Seal Families

Male seals are called **bulls**. Female seals are **cows**. A baby seal is a **pup**.

Did you know?

A seal pup drinks milk from its mother.

When a pup is born, its mother sniffs it. Then she can find it by its smell.

Food

Seals eat fish and squid. They dive down underwater to catch their food. The sea can be dark. **Whiskers** help seals feel their way around.

Seals can dive down about 1,500 feet (457 meters) underwater.

Hunted Seals

Polar bears and killer whales eat seals. So do sharks and walruses. Some people hunt seals for their meat or fur, too.

Did you know?

Some seals can hold their breath for 2 hours.

In Danger?

There are 18 kinds, or **species**, of seals. Some species are in danger. That means there are very few left.

Did you know?

There are very few Hawaiian monk seals left.

They need more food and living space. Some seal species are protected by people.

Seals look fun and friendly. But they are wild. They are important animals. They are part of a healthy ocean.

Did you know?

Seals live for about 30 years.

GLOSSARY

bulls (BULLZ): Male seals are called bulls.

cows (KOWZ): Female seals are called cows.

flippers (FLIP-purz): Flippers are webbed limbs that some animals have instead of arms and legs. Flippers help seals swim in the sea and move on land.

haul-out (HALL-owt): When a herd of seals goes on land, it is called a haul-out.

herd (HURD): A group of seals is called a herd.

molting (MOLT-ing): When a seal sheds last year's fur and skin, it is called molting.

pup (PUP): A baby seal is called a pup.

species (SPEE-sheez): A type of a certain animal. There are 18 species of seals.

whiskers (WISS-kurz): Whiskers are long, stiff hairs near an animal's mouth. Whiskers help animals feel their way around.

TO LEARN MORE

On the Web

Visit our Web page for lots of links about seals:

www.childsworld.com/links

Note to parents, teachers, and librarians: We routinely verify our Web links to make sure they are safe, active sites—so encourage your readers to check them out!

In the Library

Butterworth, Christine. *See What a Seal Can Do.* Somerville, MA: Candlewick Press, 2013.

Hendrix, Emilia. *Seals and Pups*. New York, NY: Gareth Stevens Publishing, 2016.

Meister, Cari. *Seals*. Minneapolis, MN: Jump!, 2013.

INDEX

About the Author

Kara L. Laughlin is an artist and writer who lives in Virginia with her husband, three kids, two guinea pigs, and a dog. She is the author of two dozen nonfiction books for kids.